JESUS CHRIST TO THE RESCUE

JESUS CHRIST
TO THE RESCUE

CATHERINE MACKENZIE

CF4·K

10 9 8 7 6 5 4 3 2 1

ISBN 978-1-84550-973-6

Published in 2012 by
Christian Focus Publications,
Geanies House, Fearn, Tain, Ross-shire, IV20 1TW, Scotland, U.K.

Cover design by Daniel van Straaten
Illustrations by Fred Apps
Printed in China

If you confess with your mouth that Jesus is Lord and believe in your heart that God raised him from the dead, you will be saved.

Romans 10:9

JESUS RESCUES HIS PEOPLE

If your house was on fire you would need a fire engine. The siren would sound and you would soon be rescued. Jesus rescues. He saves his

people from sin. This is what God the Father sent him to do – because the sin in our lives, our disobedience to God, is harmful to us.

Jesus rescued the disciples one day from a violent storm. The waves beat the ship and soon it was nearly sinking. Jesus was asleep at the

back of the boat. He was woken by the disciples. 'Don't you care about us,' they cried.

Jesus told the sea to be still and quiet. The wind stopped and all was calm. The disciples were safe. They were amazed at what Jesus had done. 'Who is this man? Even the wind and the waves obey him!'

But the disciples didn't always remember Jesus' love and care for them.

You can read about Jesus calming the storm in Matthew chapter 8, Mark chapter 4, and Luke chapter 8.

One disciple, Judas, told Jesus' enemies where to find him.

Another disciple, Peter, said that he would always be Jesus' friend.

But when Jesus was arrested, Peter pretended that he didn't know Jesus at all.

The story of Jesus' death can be read in all four Gospels.

Jesus was taken away to be questioned. He was then whipped and beaten by the soldiers. A crown of thorns was put on his head. He

His enemies took him to a place called Calvary. He was nailed to a cross and killed.

Jesus had never sinned, yet it was part of God the Father's plan that his Son should die.

was made fun of and people told lies about him. Jesus knew that he had been sent to save his people from their sins.

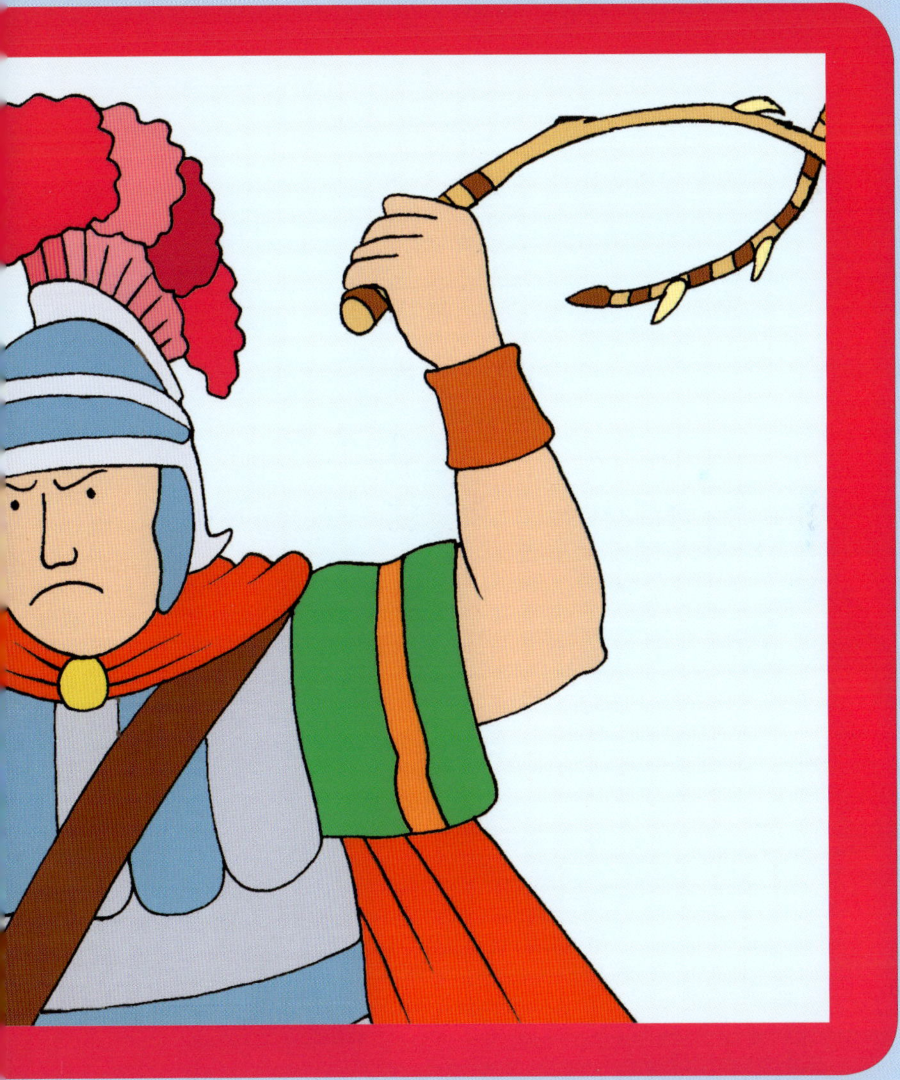

Jesus died so that those who believe in him can be rescued from sin. Jesus can forgive the wrong things that you do. He can do this because

he died on the cross. You need to be rescued from sin. Ask Jesus to rescue you today.

For everyone who calls on the name of the Lord will be saved (Romans 10:13).

JESUS HELPS HIS PEOPLE

If you fell and broke your leg, you would need an ambulance. Doctors and nurses would rush to help you. Jesus helps us. Jesus saves his people

from sin. This is what God the Father sent him to do – because the sin in our lives, our disobedience to God, is harmful to us.

Lots of people needed Jesus to help them. Sick people needed to be healthy. Blind people needed to see. Lame people needed to walk. Dead

You can read about many people who were healed by Jesus in Luke 6:17-19.

people needed to be raised to life again. Jesus did all these amazing things. Jesus helped them.

Even Roman soldiers needed help sometimes. One of them had a servant that he cared about deeply.

The servant was sick and about to die. Jesus went to help the soldier, but just before he left a messenger arrived.

You can read the story of the centurion's servant in Matthew chapter 8 and Luke chapter 7.

The soldier's message said, 'I am not good enough for you to visit me. I am not good enough to come and

visit you. Please just say the word and my servant will be healed.' Jesus healed the servant there and then.

When Jesus was arrested, other Roman soldiers hit him and hurt him. They made fun of him and Pilate,

the Roman governor, did nothing to help him.

The story of Pilate can be read in all four Gospels.

However, one Roman soldier saw Jesus die on the cross and he believed

The story of the centurion at the cross can be read in Matthew chapter 27, Mark chapter 15 and Luke 23.

that Jesus was the Son of God. Jesus had been sent to save him.

It is because Jesus is the perfect Son of God that sinners can be saved. If you believe in Jesus you will be saved from sin. You need Jesus to help you. Without him you

Believe in the Lord Jesus, and you will be saved, you and your household (Acts 16:31).

are helpless, but he is a great help. Jesus took the punishment for sin when he died on the cross at Calvary. Ask him to help you now.

JESUS SAVES HIS PEOPLE

If a robber broke into your house you would need a policeman. He would come to arrest the robber and save you.

Jesus saves. Jesus saves sinners who disobey God.

This is what God the Father sent him to do because the sin in our lives, our disobedience to God, is harmful to us.

Many people wanted to find out about Jesus. Zacchaeus climbed a tree to get a better view of him as he

walked by. Jesus saved Zacchaeus. Zacchaeus was sorry for his sin.

You can read about Zacchaeus in Luke chapter 19.

Nicodemus wanted to ask Jesus some questions. Nicodemus was scared to be seen speaking to Jesus so he came at night when it was dark.

Jesus told Nidodemus that God the Father had sent him, his only Son. Whoever believed in Jesus would have a life that never ended.

Nicodemus realised that he needed the new life that Jesus could give him. He knew that he needed to trust in him. Then one day he would go to heaven to live forever with Jesus.

When Jesus' enemies were angry with him, Nicodemus spoke up for

Jesus. But Jesus' enemies arrested him and killed him.

The story of Nicodemus can be read in John chapter 3, 7 and 19.

Later on Nicodemus helped to take Jesus' body down from the cross. They laid his body in a tomb in a garden.

Later, Mary discovered that Jesus was alive! He had risen from the dead.

Jesus was punished for sin even though he had never done anything wrong.

But Jesus had to suffer and die so that his people would be free from sin. Then they would live with him in heaven forever.

Do you love Jesus? Do you trust in him? You should. If you trust in Jesus you will be saved from sin – and you need to be saved.

For God so loved the world, that he gave his only Son, that whoever believes in him should not perish but have eternal life (John 3:16).

JESUS FINDS HIS PEOPLE

If you were lost on a mountain you would need to be found. The mountain rescue team would come to find you.

Jesus finds. Jesus finds and saves lost people. Their sin has taken them

away from God and they need to be brought back. This is what God the Father sent Jesus to do – because the sin in our lives, our disobedience to God, is harmful to us.

Often people don't know how to be happy. They are sad. To be truly happy you must love God with all

your heart. Jesus wanted to bring people back to God so they would be full of joy.

Some people wanted to have the good things that Jesus offered, but they didn't want to love God with all their hearts. They wanted to live forever, but they didn't want Jesus

to be in charge of their lives. The rich young ruler didn't want to give up his money, so he chose to keep it for himself and didn't follow Jesus.

You can read about the rich young ruler in Matthew chapter 19, Mark chapter 10 and Luke chapter 18.

However, a poor woman called Mary loved Jesus so much that she poured very expensive perfume on him. The

beautiful smell spread through the whole house.

Some people said, 'What a waste of money.' But Jesus told them to leave Mary alone. Jesus knew that

she had done this because she loved him with all her heart.

The story of the woman with the jar of perfume can be read in all four Gospels.

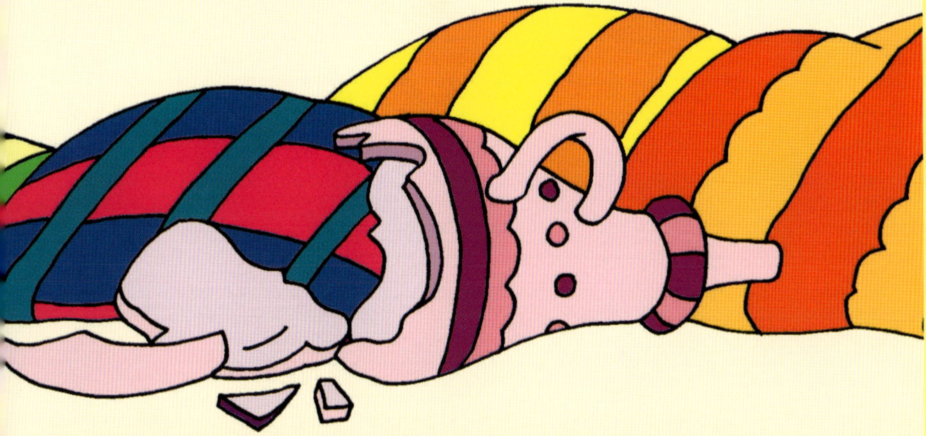

On the cross other women watched as Jesus died. They saw where he was buried. On the third day another

Mary came to the tomb and saw that his body wasn't there. Jesus spoke to her and she knew that he was alive!

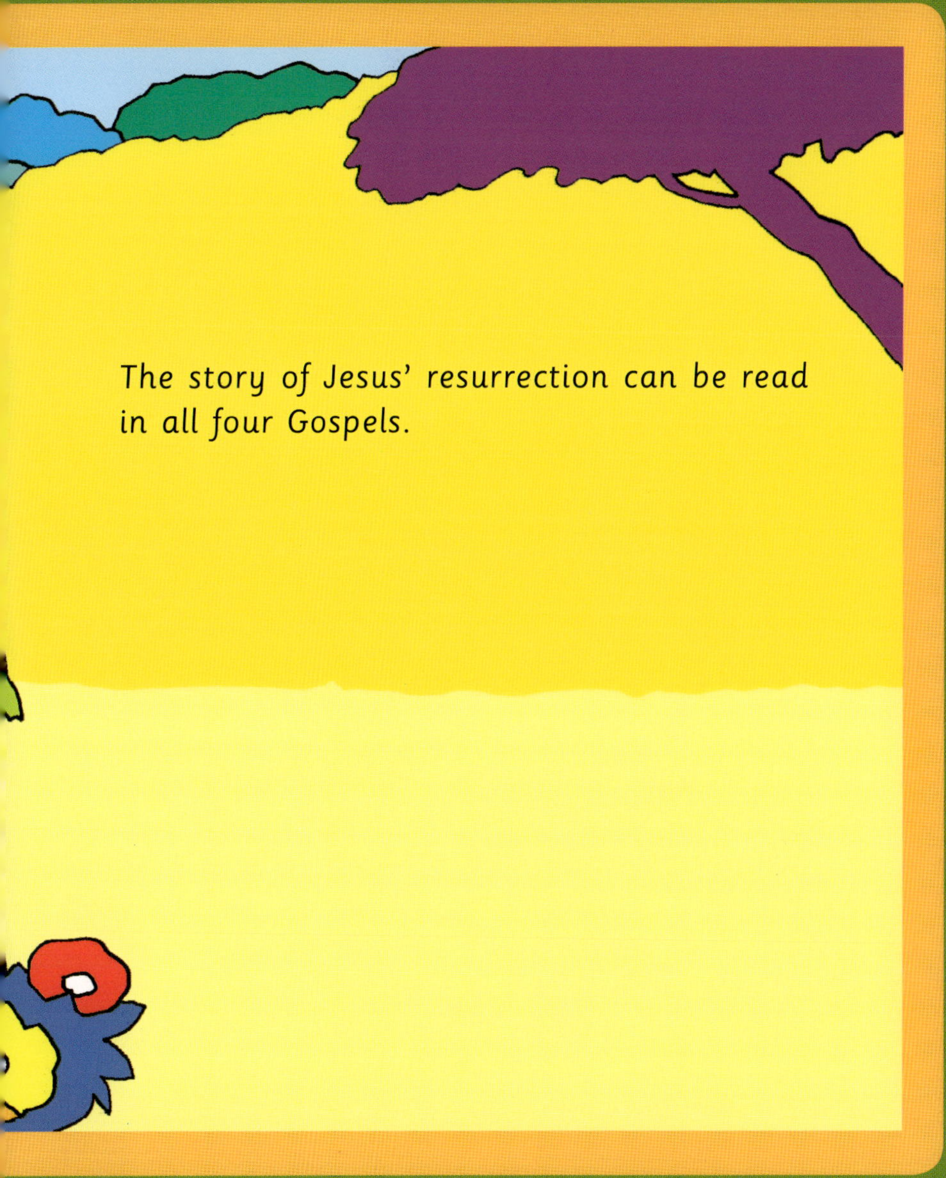

The story of Jesus' resurrection can be read in all four Gospels.

Jesus died to save his people from their sin. Then he rose to life again! This is part of God the Father's plan to save sinners. If you haven't asked

God to forgive you for your sins then you are lost, but God knows where you are. He will save you if you ask him to.

For the Son of Man came to seek and to save the lost (Luke 19:10).

CHRISTIAN FOCUS PUBLICATIONS

Christian Focus | Christian Heritage | CF4K | Mentor

Christian Focus Publications publishes books for adults and children under its four main imprints: Christian Focus, CF4K, Mentor and Christian Heritage. Our books reflect our conviction that God's Word is reliable and Jesus is the way to know him, and live for ever with him.

Our children's publication list includes a Sunday School curriculum that covers pre-school to early teens, and puzzle and activity books. We also publish personal and family devotional titles, biographies and inspirational stories that children will love.

If you are looking for quality Bible teaching for children then we have an excellent range of Bible stories and age-specific theological books.

From pre-school board books to teenage apologetics, we have it covered!

Find us at our web page:
www.christianfocus.com

CF4•K
Because you're never too young to know Jesus